SQUIRREL
IN YOUR GARDEN

DOREEN KING

Photographs: Doreen and Michael King

KINGDOM

CONTENTS

The author and publishers thank
The National Trust, Brownsea Island
for the photograph of the Red Squirrel on page 7

t.f.h.
KINGDOM

CHAPTER 1

Introducing the
SQUIRREL

Everyone recognises the squirrel. This small, attractive creature, with its very distinctive bushy tail, is often seen scampering around our gardens from about an hour after sunrise until an hour or two before dusk. It is a delight to watch it rushing up and down the trees, and it is especially appealing when it sits bolt upright on its hind legs and looks directly at you.

Most animals like to play and the squirrel is no exception. It will dart about on its own, rolling over and turning round and round to chase its own tail. Youngsters play together, chasing each other up and down the trees.

Squirrels can vocalise with a range of grunts and squeaks, growling, chattering and scolding. A frightened squirrel or a youngster calling for its mother can give a surprisingly loud squeak. A flicking tail indicates danger or acts as a greeting or warning-off signal to another squirrel. Tree slapping with the feet is another sign of a disturbed squirrel. A side-to-side swishing of the tail usually means that the squirrel is unsure of the situation.

It might be helpful to begin by placing the squirrel within the animal world.

Since there are more than a million different species of animal on our planet, many of which resemble each other to a considerable extent, we need to be able to classify these species in an ordered, scientific way. The Swedish naturalist, Carolus

Our squirrels have many cousins, including the Souslik, a ground squirrel from Russia.

A baby Grey Squirrel, its eyes not yet open.

Linnaeus, developed the Binomial System of Nomenclature for this purpose in the 18th century. According to this system, creatures are divided into Classes, one of which groups together creatures which suckle their young and is known as **Mammalia,** or Mammals. The Classes are then subdivided into Orders, and among the Mammals are such orders as **Carnivora** (meat-eaters like cats and dogs) and **Primates** (so-called *highest* or *prime* order, including monkeys, apes and man). Like rats and voles, squirrels are mammals belonging to the order **Rodentia** (rodents – meaning gnawing animals). In turn, the order Rodentia is subdivided into families (**Sciuridae** in the case of squirrels). These in turn are divided into genera (singular: genus), which is *Sciurus* for squirrels (fittingly meaning *tail shadow*), and then again into species. A species is defined by two names (hence the *binomial system*), one indicating the genus and the other a specific name. There are only two species of squirrel found in Britain, *Sciurus vulgaris* (the Red Squirrel) and *Sciurus carolinensis* (the Eastern North American Grey Squirrel).

There are 267 species of squirrel, a surprisingly large number considering that

Notes

A Grey Squirrel

Britain only has Red and Grey Squirrels. The Chipmunk, Marmot and Souslik are types of squirrel. In fact, squirrels can be divided into three types: tree squirrels, flying squirrels and ground squirrels. The two species found in Britain are tree squirrels.

There are no Red Squirrels in Southern or Central England except on the Isle of Wight and Brownsea Island in Poole Harbour. However, they can be seen in parts of Europe, and in temperate Asia as far as Japan. Indeed, the Red Squirrel is sometimes called the Common Squirrel as, whilst its numbers are low in Britain, it is a common sight in Europe, and certainly not an endangered species.

The Grey Squirrel is very common in Britain. It can be seen in most parts of England, and in large areas of Scotland and Ireland. It is often called the American Grey and sometimes the American Eastern North Grey or the Eastern Grey. There are several different species of squirrel that are grey, which can be confusing.

Grey Squirrels were introduced into Britain in 1876 when Mr Brocklehurst released a pair into Henbury Park in Cheshire. There followed many introductions up until about the turn of the century, including a number of different species. However, it is the Eastern North American Grey Squirrel *(Sciurus carolinensis)* that has thrived so well and become established in Britain.

A Red Squirrel. Note the tufted ears. Now rare in England, it is still common in Europe.

A Red Squirrel. In southern Britain, these can now be seen in the wild only on the Isle of Wight and Brownsea Island.

The cheeky Chipmunk is another squirrel common in North America.

Characteristics

Grey Squirrels are much more likely to be seen than Reds, as they spend much more time on the ground. In general Red Squirrels have colouring to match the pine/spruce/fir forests in which they are traditionally found, and Grey Squirrels have colouring to match the beech trees in which they live.

- The Red Squirrel has bright chestnut brown fur on its upper parts. It may have some grey fur on its flanks and head. It has ear tufts which are particularly noticeable in winter.
- The Grey Squirrel has grey upper parts and it may have some chestnut brown on its lower flanks and head. Grey Squirrels do not have ear tufts.

The Red and Grey Squirrel both have white underparts. They are most easily distinguishable by the absence of ear tufts in the Grey Squirrel. Furthermore,

The Marmot, also called a Woodchuck, is a North American ground squirrel.

A young male Grey Squirrel

A mature female Grey Squirrel. Note the four pairs of teats.

An adult Grey Squirrel in captivity playing in its cage.

the Grey Squirrel is much larger. Nevertheless, Grey Squirrels sometimes have a fair quantity of reddish fur, and Red Squirrels of grey fur, so the two species can be confused. Also, there are some colour variations: black Grey Squirrels can occur, while albinos are found in Red and Grey Squirrels.

Both species moult twice yearly, in spring and autumn, becoming darker in colour during the winter months. The moult may take a couple of months to complete. They both put on weight to get them through the winter, too, but the Grey puts on rather more than the Red (about 25% more for the Grey and 12% more for the Red). The weight varies as follows:

- Red Summer: 260g   Winter: 285g
- Grey Summer: 480g   Winter: 600g

They do not hibernate, but become inactive during very cold weather, only coming out of their home for a couple of hours each day.

CHAPTER 1

Notes

Grey Squirrels can often be seen in urban parks, begging for food. They can become extremely tame.

The normal body temperature of a squirrel is 37–40°C. This falls a few degrees at night, and they sun-bathe during the day to warm themselves.

Squirrels have four toes on the front feet with a small 'thumb', and five toes on the back feet. Their claws are very sharp, enabling them to scale trees and walls with ease. They can jump and swim and are generally very agile. Their trademark, of course, is the large bushy tail, which they hold upright across their backs when sitting. They also have large eyes and sharp teeth.

In female squirrels, the genitals are close to the tail and they have four pairs of teats. The vulva becomes pink and swollen during œstrous and the female is usually receptive on one day only. In males, the penis is about 1cm away from the anus. The scrotum, which is situated between the penis and anus, grows as the testes descend during breeding season. Out of breeding season the testes shrink.

Squirrels are thought to have colour vision, but they cannot distinguish red from green. In my opinion they have poor close-range vision.

Squirrels and people

In general, the squirrel is very popular. Many people visit parks especially to feed squirrels, and children particularly love to do this. Where people feed them regularly squirrels become quite tame, taking peanuts from the hand. They expect to be fed, and sit waiting patiently for you to find your peanuts. They look as though they are begging for food when they squat upright and hold up their front feet to take the food. They do not usually run onto you, but tame ones might if they think you have some food for them. They may also follow you if you feed them.

Squirrels have adapted very well to living with humans, and parks are not their only habitat. As well as in farmland, forests, and parks, squirrels live in gardens that have trees. They can also live in the middle of towns, making their homes in street trees and, given the opportunity, even in houses. I have seen squirrels successfully raise families in chimney pots and crevices in high walls. They do not usually raid domestic rubbish bags as, being agile, they can help themselves to anything tasty that has been thrown into an open litter bin. I frequently see squirrels running along the pavement on my way to work; they are common in the parks and streets of London.

When you feed squirrels, they usually eat some of the food you give them and bury the rest. They quickly dig little holes, and peanuts will soon be buried all around the garden. No-one who feeds squirrels can help wondering whether they will remember where they buried all those nuts. In most cases they don't! In times of shortage they hunt for buried food by smell. Burying nuts is akin to planting trees, so the squirrel does its bit for conservation. However, it has also been blamed for killing trees because it likes to eat the sap layer. It also raids the nests of birds.

Although the Grey Squirrel is considered to be a pest under government policy, most people enjoy seeing it because it is one of the few wild animals to be seen in Britain during the day (diurnal), and also because it is an attractive and mischievous. Its antics can be very entertaining, as it is cheeky and bold. It is especially enchanting when it sits up and eats its food, using its front feet like hands. Consequently, many people like to understand about their garden squirrel and to enjoy its company. An understanding of the squirrel's needs is particularly important in the case of the Red Squirrel as it may soon disappear from Britain.

A SQUIRREL'S *life*

It is delightful to see squirrels playing in the garden, scampering around and making spectacular leaps of up to six metres. They are generally inoffensive and never bite unless you attempt to handle them. Even if one crawls up your arm those very sharp claws seldom scratch.

Feeding

The Grey Squirrel's favourite source of food is the deciduous tree; it eats nuts, fruits, berries, sap and buds. Grey Squirrels also consume small quantities of green foods such as shoots and flowers, hips, roots, wheat, maize, fungi, invertebrates, birds' eggs and young birds. They also dig up and eat bulbs. Unlike Red Squirrels, Greys rarely live in coniferous forests.

As well as all the things that Grey Squirrels eat, Reds enjoy the cones of such coniferous trees as the Scots pine, larch, fir and spruce.

Tree squirrels prefer to live in mature forests, and Grey Squirrels like hazel and beech nuts. In broad-leaved forests Red Squirrels eat mainly hazel nuts. Unlike their grey cousins they do not rely on buried food, so Grey Squirrels have an advantage when there is a food shortage. Red Squirrels spend most of their time feeding in trees, whereas Greys will spend a large proportion of their time on the ground.

Squirrels are fussy about the nuts they eat, willingly spending precious time and energy opening a nut if they think it contains a seed that is in good condition. They turn nuts over and over in their paws to test the weight before deciding whether they are worth cracking. Squirrels seem able to tell; they rarely open bad nuts.

Acorn

Scots pine cone

Common hazel bud

Hip

This very happy squirrel has just conducted a successful raid on the bird table.

Grey Squirrels seem more adaptable, scavenging for all sorts of 'human' food in towns, as mentioned previously. When they bury food it is called a *cache,* and each cache may contain several food items. Individual squirrels probably cannot remember where they buried their own food, but they can smell food. They search

Sycamore

Beech nut

Hazel nut

Sweet chestnut

and find caches, although the caches found may be those made by another squirrel.

Some squirrels, though not the Reds and Greys found in Britain, form *middens*. These are larders of food – storage sites used by squirrels when food is hard to find.

Predation and death

Squirrels can live for up to ten years in captivity but the life expectancy of a wild squirrel is only about five years.

It is just as well that squirrels are very agile, as most carnivores will eat them if they can catch them. Pine martins and snakes eat them when they can. Foxes, cats and dogs kill them if they can catch them. Badgers, stoats, weasels, owls, polecats and wild cats also have a taste for them, but these nocturnal predators normally hunt near the ground, so are not a serious threat. Large birds sometimes eat the young, and hawks can take adult squirrels.

In towns the cat is one of their worst enemies. Cats can catch squirrels that do not get off the ground quickly enough. From the numbers of casualties brought to me, I would suggest that the cat may be a significant controlling factor for urban squirrel populations. Another one is the motor car. Squirrels are frequently killed by cars as they tend to dash across roads like cats do. The juveniles are at greater risk from cats, dogs and cars. Many squirrels are poisoned, both deliberately by humans and by eating foods that do not agree with them, and they are frequently killed by falling from trees onto concrete pavements. Yes, they do sometimes fall, usually on the head, hurting themselves badly.

However, the major controlling factors for the Grey Squirrel population at large are thought to be food supply and the availability of trees. Weather conditions, predation, disease and human intervention may all have some effect. Only about 50% of young squirrels survive their first year and the figure can be much lower in bad years. It is thought that starvation when they leave the nest in the summer is a major factor. The inexperienced squirrel also has to learn how to build a drey. When they first disperse from the nest, they often use existing dreys. Their first attempts at building dreys can be very poor and they die of exposure if the weather is bad. Some may succumb to diseases. The two major diseases that have been studied are coccidiosis and parapoxvirus.

Squirrels can swim but they cannot cope with getting too cold. They are seldom far from their dreys on cold, wet days.

Breeding

The breeding season is from about February until September (mainly May until August), one or two broods being raised each year. Squirrels usually moult just before and just after the breeding season.

During January and February male courtship displays can be seen. The male flicks his tails and slaps the tree with his front paws, chattering loudly. Courtship ends with a chase. The female is chased up and down the trees (possibly by a procession of males one after the other) until she is ready to mate. She is usually receptive on one day only for the first brood, and one day only for the second brood. There have been reports of Red Squirrels having more than two broods.

Gestation (pregnancy) is about 38 days for the Red Squirrel and 44 for the Grey. From one to six young may be born, but the average litter size is three. The young (called *pinkies* at this stage) are born blind, naked and deaf, and they are cared for by the mother only. If disturbed, the mother may move her babies to a new home.

At three-and-a-half weeks the eyes and ears of the young squirrels are open, they have fur, and their teeth are beginning to show. At this age Reds weigh about 50g and Greys about 90g. At about seven weeks they venture out of the nest and they should be fully weaned by about eight weeks. At this stage Reds should weigh about 150g and Greys about 280g. At 10 to 14 weeks they are fully independent and start to disperse. Young Grey Squirrels leaving the nest can travel up to 8km within a few days.

The young squirrels are slightly smaller than the adults and can be distinguished by their tails. In a young squirrel the tail is not so fluffy, and it is not held up quite correctly in the characteristic position across the back. The tails are also thin, often with kinks in them. The young become sexually mature at about one year old. You can tell if a squirrel is less than 30 to 40 days old because squirrels do not usually start to groom themselves until this age.

Nests

Squirrels sleep in nests called dreys and dens. They are adaptable, and Grey Squirrels make their dens in holes in trees and walls, lofts, chimney pots, cavity walls, bird boxes, and anywhere else that offers some protection from the rain. In general, the den is an adapted hollow. The former nests of birds such as woodpeckers are often used. Grey Squirrels will also nest on the ground in old rabbit or rat burrows.

A drey is an open, domed nest, usually situated high up in the fork of a tree. It is about 0.3m across and the base is made from twigs, often fresh ones with the leaves still attached. In any wood noted for its squirrels, virtually every tree houses a drey. Squirrels use bark for the roofs. Dreys can also be found in bushes, but these

Squirrels will live quite happily in holes in the trunks of trees. Such homes are called *dens*.

are usually the nests of juvenile squirrels that have been unable to sleep in trees because there are too many well established squirrels in the area.

Squirrels make spherical nests in which to sleep out of grass, moss, hair, and anything else, such as tissue, wool, paper rags and feathers, that takes their fancy. Keeping warm appears to be a problem for them. They sleep curled into a ball with their tails over their heads. The winter nests are usually much more substantial than the summer ones.

Squirrels usually have more than one nest in use at any one time, and they swap between dens or dreys every few days. Nest sharing occurs, but they tend only to share with squirrels they know. Two sharing is common, but more may share, especially in cold weather, when they huddle together to keep each other warm.

In general, Red Squirrels tend to nest in dreys and are not so imaginative with their nesting sites as Greys. Grey Squirrels tend to be a little more sociable and may be seen in groups at feeding sites.

Living together

Although some squirrels are a little territorial, the British Red and Grey Squirrels are not territorial animals. However, a mother will defend the vicinity of her drey. They have a range (an area in which the animal can usually be found). However, other squirrels may live in the same area.

There is a pecking order, and strange squirrels are chased away. This means that youngsters are usually chased away from the best ranges, especially if they do not make themselves known to the neighbours when they are still with the mother. Resident squirrels can be particularly aggressive to 'immigrants' and, as the pecking order is weight dependent, the young squirrels usually fare the worst.

Dispersal of young squirrels usually occurs in the autumn. At this time the young squirrels move more than a kilometre away to settle in a home range. This time of year is associated with road casualties. It should be noted that many young squirrels simply radiate out gradually from the nest, so that they are known to neighbouring squirrels; dispersing squirrels are treated as immigrants in new populations. Squirrels are sociable animals. They do sometimes fight although seldom to the death. They scent-mark their favourite routes by urinating and face-wiping.

On sensing danger, squirrels watch from a safe distance or disappear from sight.

They are very sensitive animals, with acute hearing and vision. For this reason they are easily startled and frightened by people, although they are basically friendly.

A SQUIRREL-
friendly garden

Garden design

If you want to keep your garden squirrels happy, you must consider their likes and dislikes. They may come to your garden to drink from your pond, to feed, to nest in the bird box and to take moss and leaves to line their dreys. Once they discover the bird peanut feeders, you will have regular squirrel visitors.

Squirrels are quick and very active. They like to climb and play in trees and to dig in the earth. They travel around and may visit many gardens during a day. Fences and walls will not deter them; in fact they like to climb up and down them. Neither will they be deterred by people, as long as they are not frightened by sudden and loud noises that they are not accustomed to hearing. Squirrel families raised near roads will be used to traffic.

Squirrels enjoy foraging in bushy areas of gardens. However, they also like closely-cut grass and areas such as dense woodland where the ground cover is sparse. Consequently they are at home in the well-tended garden that has some trees.

Water and food in a garden will attract a wide range of wildlife, and you should allow for this when you consider the use of insecticides.

Squirrels are active and inquisitive. Their aerobatics are a pleasure to watch.

Insecticides deplete natural food supplies and make creatures such as birds, hedgehogs and squirrels very ill, possibly killing them. Some common plants such as foxgloves and lupins are also poisonous, and squirrels (and children!) can become very ill if they eat these, too.

By all means plant your roses and beans, but also plant holly or other evergreen shrubs. Eat your lettuces and blackberries, but leave a few for the garden residents. Keep your ornamental fish pond with your prize goldfish, but leave a wildlife pond for frogs, hedgehogs and squirrels. Squirrels need frequent drinks and will help themselves at the bird bath.

A gardener's aim is usually to make the garden as attractive and interesting as possible. What could enhance a beautiful, well-cultivated garden more than a wide selection of wildlife to watch?

If you have a reasonably large garden and really want to attract wildlife, plant a tree. Trees provide not only shade, beauty and oxygenated air for us to breathe, but also homes and food for a wide range of wildlife. The oak, a native tree, supports many creatures: mammals, birds and insects. It is beautiful and offers a shady spot in the garden. Grey Squirrels particularly like hazel and beech trees.

Trees should not be planted too close to the house because the roots and over-hanging branches might cause damage. Your nursery can probably advise you about planting distances for individual trees, but generally you should not plant a forest tree within 5m of your house. Special consideration is needed when planting sycamore trees, because they have very long roots. Bear in mind that all trees need a certain amount of care.

Large forest trees are not suitable for small urban gardens. Instead, choose dwarf and semi-dwarf trees or trees that naturally remain quite small. I favour fruit trees because I like my garden to be productive as well as attractive.

Feeding squirrels

Squirrels soon become accustomed to being fed. If you feed them at a particular time each day you may find them waiting for you. They always seem eager to take food, but they need it most during the winter months and in the middle of summer, when the ground is hard. You may not see them regularly during the winter, as they become inactive and sleepy during the day, but they come out for food when they wake up. Young squirrels can become dependent, so aim to feed them regularly. Preferably feed them every few days; this allows the summer youngsters to learn how to find food for themselves. Squirrels, especially youngsters, are vulnerable to starvation in the summer, before nuts become plentiful.

As I mentioned previously, squirrels, especially Greys, eat a wide range of food. Although they have keen senses of sight and smell, they do not seem able to sense food from more than 30m away. However, they usually come eagerly if you gain their attention by calling them.

Most people feed squirrels on peanuts. Unshelled ones can be offered from the hand. They also take the shelled ones, but it is best to avoid giving them salted peanuts.

Squirrel tables can be attached to any tree or bush. Avoid placing them on the ground away from trees because it makes it easier for cats to kill the squirrels when they come to feed.

Some people have made a special hobby of devising elaborate feeding equipment and assault courses for squirrels. Squirrels can be trained to climb along ropes, leap, and spring onto levers to get their peanuts. They learn these tricks from watching other squirrels perform them. You can gradually increase the complexity of the assault course over a period of months, or even years. In a study at the London Zoo, Regent's Park, feeders were supplied that only Red Squirrels could use because they were selective upon the weight of the animal. Even so, a few diligent Grey Squirrels overcame the problem by learning to balance on their front paws only.

Large trees like this one are irresistible to playful squirrels.

Squirrels eat most types of nuts, but do not give them 'conkers' from the horse chestnut tree. Tree seeds such as acorns, beech, hazel and hornbeam are taken, but I do not recommend giving squirrels such food, as unripe seeds can be poisonous. I am thinking in particular of acorns. Green acorns are poisonous and sensible squirrels avoid them.

Squirrels are particularly fond of chocolate and ice-cream. They also eat biscuits and dried fruit. Bread and fresh fruit are taken only when the squirrels are particularly hungry. Squirrels always accept peanuts and other nuts; if they are not hungry they will store the food, possibly burying it in front of you.

Water

Water can be a very attractive feature in a garden, and squirrels are not the only creatures that will thank you for it. A water supply is particularly welcome in the hot, dry summer months. During other times of the year squirrels will obtain most of the moisture they need from their food.

The wildlife pond with gently sloping sides is most suitable, as traditional ornamental ponds with steep sides can be fatal. Squirrels can swim, and they usually manage to clamber out of ponds with steep sides, but most wild creatures prefer ponds that are easily accessible to them. Ornamental ponds can be made more wildlife-friendly by adding flower-pots at the sides to form ledges.

If there is no pond in your garden, you can fill an upturned dustbin lid or similar container with water and leave it at ground level for your thirsty garden visitors. It should be cleaned out regularly.

Nesting sites

As has already been said, squirrels like to nest high up in oaks and other large forest trees. If the trees in the area are not to their liking, or have already been claimed by other squirrels, they will nest in houses, offices and factories. Chimney pots, lofts (not recommended!) and holes in high walls are popular sites.

Squirrels are adept at raiding bird nesting boxes if the entrance is not reinforced with metal. They sometimes nest in the larger bird boxes, and can squeeze through quite small holes.

'The birds' loss is my gain!'

Squirrel-friendly gardening

Squirrels do not usually have too many accidents in the garden. They seldom drown in ponds because they are good swimmers and can usually climb out. They do sometimes get caught in garden wire, and their frantic efforts to get free can result in the most horrific injuries. It is best never to leave netting and wire lying around.

The predominant danger to squirrels is poisoning. They sample a wide range of food, and what they eat does not always agree with them. Weed killers, insecticides and slug pellets can make them seriously ill, possibly killing them. Any substance that is likely to be harmful to birds and bees will probably harm squirrels too.

There are times when you need to control garden pests and weeds, particularly with food crops. However, there are alternatives to chemicals. Refer to a good gardening book and you will find descriptions of age-old methods, including:

* leaving a jar of beer to kill the slugs
* keeping slugs out by planting rows of chives around vegetable beds
* keeping the greenfly away by spraying roses with soapy water
* hoeing regularly rather than spraying for weed control. (Your garden robin will be appreciative of your hoeing, too!)
* mulches are good for weed control

Friend or foe?

Although most people enjoy seeing squirrels, the Grey Squirrel is regarded officially as a pest. It certainly raids bird nests and strips bark from trees. I have not seen squirrels kill any of my local trees, but there have been claims that squirrels can affect the timber trade significantly by bark stripping. They peel it off to eat the sap layer below, also enjoying fungus growing under the bark, and sometimes the bark itself. If they strip a layer of bark right around the trunk and eat the sap layer, the tree will die, because its plumbing system has been destroyed and no nutrients can pass up the trunk. The tree is said to have been *girdled*.

Where bark has been stripped, the tree is also vulnerable to attack by fungi and insects. This could result in the tree forming calluses detrimental to the timber value. Squirrels prefer trees that have thick sap layers, which usually means young trees that are growing well. Bark stripping is often worse when there is a good breeding season coupled with a good tree-growing season.

It is worth mentioning that many other animals remove bark from trees. Hares, rabbits, deer and cattle all eat bark. Bears and dormice eat the unlignified tissue (the sap layer) beneath the bark.

There have been many debates about why squirrels strip bark. It could be triggered by either a liking for sap or a need to divert aggression to a 'safe' activity.

My experience of Grey Squirrels suggests that they have a liking for sweet things; bark stripping may be reduced when 'sweets' and a water source are supplied. As squirrels are quite intelligent, once one squirrel starts the stripping habit, others will follow. Bark stripping is worse when there are high densities of squirrels.

Squirrels have also been accused of causing damage to arable crops, orchards, and soft fruit crops. However, any such damage is unlikely to be of economical significance. They have also been accused of taking grain left out for pheasants.

Another charge levelled against the squirrel is the murder of young birds. However, it is unlikely that squirrels are the main cause of such deaths where there are substantial populations of crows and magpies.

It is recognised by ecologists that balance in nature is essential, and that one link in the food chain cannot be destroyed without affecting the whole system. Squirrels eat invertebrates and they also plant trees. Furthermore, as squirrels are so fussy about their nuts, they will endeavour to plant only the best seeds. Squirrels can also be beneficial to forests as they eat the caterpillars that cause tree death by defoliation.

Sport shooting and drey poking and shooting have little effect on total squirrel numbers. The most effective control has been by poisoning, usually using Warfarin. Unlike some countries, Great Britain has no closed season for Grey Squirrels so, when poisoning is carried out in the late spring, many baby squirrels starve. Although the Red Squirrel is a protected species in Britain, it too can be killed if a licence is granted. If there is a genuine need to control squirrel populations, the most humane and effective method is the use of chemicals to control reproduction; in other words, birth control pills! Unfortunately, further research into such chemicals is still needed.

Squirrels have traditionally been hunted for fur (squirrel pelts are often called *calabars*), food and/or sport and therefore they have a long history of being 'useful' for humans. Their meat has also been used to feed domestic pets.

Squirrels are friendly creatures who do not usually bite unless an attempt is made to pick them up. They are very inoffensive, keeping their distance while living side by side with humans. They bring an enormous amount of pleasure to gardeners, but can be a bit of a nuisance at times. However there are usually ways to counteract their efforts.

You can avoid loss of bark from your favourite ornamental tree by wrapping a sheet of metal around the trunk. This should be one metre deep and one or two metres from the ground.

In response to your hospitality the little nutkins may dig holes all over your lawn – though they do cover them up! Furthermore, they may dig up your bulbs. The large ones that are available in shops are very tempting to a hungry squirrel. So plant a few more!

If you want to keep your peanuts strictly for the birds, you can protect your bird table by mounting it on a thin metal post and siting it well away from overhanging branches. Alternatively, a metal cone can be fitted to your existing post to prevent squirrels from climbing up it, or you can wrap a one-metre-wide sheet of metal around the post. Your peanut feeds could also be hung from first floor window ledges.

Unfortunately, squirrels can be a problem in lofts. People who have squirrels in their lofts should aim to eradicate them. Squirrels are inquisitive rodents whose ever-growing teeth gnaw wood with relative ease, and they think nothing of chewing

Although squirrels do eat newly-formed buds, the damage is usually minimal.

through electric wires! I have never heard of a squirrel biting through electric cables locally but, for safety reasons, it is important you do not allow them into your loft to try. They may also use loft insulation for nesting material and chew through boxes or other items stored in the attic, and they can be very noisy tenants!

It is useless to kill the squirrels; this will only enable another squirrel family to move in. Some firms will offer to trap and remove the squirrels alive. If the animal is a Grey Squirrel, it is illegal to release it, and therefore it will probably be killed anyway.

Moth balls or other naphthalene/paradichlorobenzene products used to kill moths sometimes keep squirrels away as they dislike the smell. Copper naphthenate solutions in linseed oil have also been used to keep squirrels off wood shingles. Scent repellents can be bought from hardware stores and these have been used with mixed success. Even air freshener sprays may drive the squirrels away. However, the only long-term solution is to prevent their access to the roof space. Strong wire netting is needed. This must not be more than 25mm size mesh or the squirrel may attempt to squeeze through it. The mesh must be fixed to all access points. You must not block up your roof ventilation, which is why mesh is best.

If the access is through loose tiles, missing bricks, or rotted soffits or barge-boards, these should be repaired. Squirrels are often blamed for such damage, but they are not usually destructive, preferring to use holes that became available through lack of repair. Furthermore, squirrels will use over-hanging branches to gain access to roofs. As well as facilitating the squirrels' access, such branches lead to blockages in the

Squirrels enjoy foraging in gardens.

Squirrels are the most agile of climbers, fascinating to watch in trees.

guttering at leaf fall, so overhanging branches should be removed. The best time to carry out such repairs is mid-morning and mid-afternoon, when the squirrels are most likely to be away from their nest foraging.

The squirrels in your roof may just be adult squirrels using it as a shelter, not for raising a family. Do take special care, however, that there are no babies in the nest. Grey Squirrels may have dependent young at any time from February until September. Check the nest before you carry out any work. The female will begin to take the young out foraging when they are about seven weeks old. If you cannot wait until all the animals have left because of building works, the young will need to be removed. Remember that, when firms offer to trap squirrels, they may only catch the mother, leaving the babies to starve in your loft.

It is worth noting that, if you deliberately disturb a full drey, the mother may move her young to another nest. Be prepared to deal with the youngsters if she deserts them instead. The babies can be hand reared (see Chapter 6). Remember: the older the squirrel, the greater will be its chances of survival. Baby squirrels are usually quite easy to hand rear once their eyes are open. If you cannot hand rear them yourself you might find the address of a local wildlife helpline in your telephone directory. Alternatively, your vet may be able to put you in touch with someone willing to take them. This may be worth checking before you have them destroyed.

CHAPTER *4*

Notes

Handling and housing
SQUIRRELS

Does your garden squirrel need a helping hand?

It is usually easy to tell whether your garden squirrel needs a helping hand. Obviously you should try to free it if it has become tangled up in wire netting. Use stout gloves if you need to handle an adult squirrel (gauntlets are suitable). In this case, if possible, clip the wire with wire cutters. If you cannot cut the animal free, throw an old piece of material over the animal, put it very gently into a bucket with a lid, a plastic box, rabbit hutch, bird cage, dustbin or any other sturdy container, and take it to your vet to have it cut free.

It is usually unnecessary to confine lively squirrels; they will disappear up trees even when they are injured. However, it may be necessary to trap them if, for instance, you have to move them from an unsuitable area. When an outdoor trap is used it is best to cover it with a waterproof sheet or, preferably, supply a nest box in which the squirrel can hide. Visit traps at least twice a day.

If you pick up a youngster that is not too badly hurt, it may create a terrible fuss. If its mother hears its calls, you may see her. She, too, may create a

Handling cone

30

Squirrels are constantly watching for danger, and they often pose on three legs to look around.

terrible fuss, looking as though she is showing off. If the youngster is just a lost baby, the mother may pick it up and carry it away when you put it down and stand back.

Unfortunately, the babies found are usually past the stage of creating a fuss, being too tired and weak to do anything. It is the baby squirrel with its eyes just open that is often found in the garden. The youngster has probably fallen from its nest or got lost on its first excursion. By the time that it is found it is usually cold and hungry. Baby squirrels are often found in drain holes.

Always examine felled trees for animal and bird nests. If trees are felled in an area where squirrels are known to live, do check the tree carefully for dreys and dens; you may find a nest full of naked, blind babies. Squirrel mothers may move their families to safer accommodation if you give them a little time.

It is perfectly in order, and indeed it is humane, to care for an injured, sick or baby squirrel. However, when selecting the best possible treatment (or humane euthanasia if necessary) for the animal, remember that technically it is illegal to release Grey Squirrels in Britain. On the other hand, the Red Squirrel is a protected species. In Britain, the Department of the Environment can advise you further. It is not there to prosecute the well-intentioned public. The general aim is to protect the environment for all concerned. Consequently the staff there will be pleased to answer any questions you have and can issue a licence for the long-term captivity of a wild squirrel.

Handling

Young squirrels, which look smaller than the adults and have thin tails, usually neither bite nor struggle to escape. However, you should always wear thick gloves when picking them up for the first time.

Adult squirrels can give quite a nasty bite. They also have sharp claws for climbing and are very quick. It follows that you should not handle an adult squirrel unless it is really necessary. If the squirrel is very poorly, throw a piece of material over it. If it is quite lively, it is best to coax it into a shed or trap. You can pick it up by grabbing it around the neck and catching its front leg between your fore and middle finger. However, this will not prevent a bite and the animal, if it is not practically dead, will wiggle into all manner of contortions to try to free itself.

If you need to restrain and examine a lively squirrel then, rather than

Once their eyes are open, young squirrels become very curious – especially where food is concerned!

handling it, pop it into a handling cone (see illustration on page 30). Should you need to improvise quickly you can use a large wire bird-feeder about 5cm x 5cm x 30cm long and with blockable openings both ends. If the animal needs an injection, this is the easiest way to immobilise it safely.

Baby squirrels are usually very gentle but, once they start to feed themselves, they like to chew. If you happen to have some sugar on your finger, they may try to chew this, so do be careful with children. Furthermore, some young squirrels that are very gentle with the people they know can act rather strangely towards your visitors.

Hand-reared squirrels are very gentle explorers. They jump all over you and especially like to disappear into your pockets or under your clothes. It can be difficult to remove them, so do take care; this can be very frightening for a child. However, despite their very long claws, you will probably find that they tickle rather than scratch.

When handling squirrels remember that they are very sensitive and nervous. Sudden movements and loud cries may frighten them. I have found that lack of coordination is common in baby squirrels, but in adults it can be a symptom of stress.

Be very careful not to let your squirrel escape from you while it is a guest in your home. If it does, it may disappear inside your settee or armchair!

Bird table or squirrel table? This Grey Squirrel has its own ideas.

Housing adult squirrels

All squirrels will benefit from being kept away from bright lights and sudden noises, especially when they are first taken into care.

Although squirrels are quite sociable animals it is usually best to house adult squirrels separately. They sometimes fight and, if one is particularly weak, it could be hurt. Baby squirrels also fight sometimes, particularly if they are of different ages. You can usually house squirrels from the same litter together.

Squirrels prefer to be kept in open wire cages. If you really want a happy squirrel, add a small box for its drey. A cardboard box with a small opening can be used. Line the box with newspaper and paper towels and the squirrel will cut them into strips to form a nest. The material sold in pet shops for hamster and guinea pig nests is also suitable. Alternatively, rags can be used.

You will also have a happier squirrel if the box is raised off the ground. Squirrels like to sleep off the ground and feel intimidated if they have very low housing.

Remember that the squirrel is a gnawing animal, and it needs to gnaw to keep its teeth healthy. Give it a piece of clean, untreated wood for this purpose.

For large outside cages, it might be best to have the wire on the inside. This will help to prevent the animal from gnawing the framework. As for all animals, cages must have an area sheltered from direct sunlight.

If the cage is large enough, wooden perches can be added for the squirrel to climb up. In an open wire cage, the squirrel will also climb around using the wire. The cage can be lined with newspaper and paper towels.

Sick squirrels should be kept at a constant temperature of about 30°C. Heating pads, lamps, incubators or hot water bottles can be used. Any squirrel that feels cold to the touch should be kept warm in this way. Post-operative animals can be placed on absorbent towels. Nappies are suitable.

Squirrels under observation can be kept at room temperature (21°C), so a warm room will suffice.

Once the squirrel is recovering, it will need to be acclimatised. This means that the temperature needs to drop by a few degrees at a time. Never transfer a squirrel directly from a heated room to outside housing or it will probably die the same night. The order of transfer is: heating pads – heated room – unheated room – outdoor housing.

Housing baby squirrels

Baby squirrels less than three weeks old whose eyes are still closed should be kept in incubators or over heating pads at a constant temperature of about 30°C. Plastic containers about 60cm by 30cm are suitable. Line them with newspaper and tissue.

The container needs a lid as, once the squirrels are furred, they are liable to climb. The babies should be given a plastic teddy as a comforter and loosely covered with tissue, rags or bubble film.

As the babies become more mobile it is a good idea to divide the container into two parts. Put nesting material in one, to be the sleeping compartment, and line the other with newspaper, on which the food and water bowls can be placed. This will help to keep the sleeping area clean and dry.

I still find it best to keep them on heating pads until they begin to become more active during the day, even after their eyes have opened. This is because they seem to get cold very quickly. I use heating pads at night until the squirrels can feed themselves. A very young squirrel sleeps most of the day, waking up when it is hungry. It will curl up and tuck itself away to keep warm. Squirrels that become cold are likely to die, so it is best to be on the safe side and keep them warm. They may alternate between periods of intense activity and periods of sleep, when they cool down very quickly. Squirrels urinate copiously, especially while on milk, so take special care that they are warm and not lying on wet, cold material.

In the wild, young squirrels dive into the drey from the top.

Baby squirrels get cold very easily. This one has snuggled up to conserve heat.

Once the squirrel can feed itself, then house it like the adult squirrels, but keep a close eye on it initially to ensure that it does not get cold.

Squirrels kept in outdoor housing should be treated regularly for parasites.

Transporting squirrels

Adult squirrels can be transported in their cages. Baby squirrels are happiest in small containers that can serve as dreys. They will then sleep through the journey. Baby squirrels can easily become accustomed to being transported in this way, and will not mind at all.

Treating the
SQUIRREL

In my experience there are three main groups of squirrels needing care:
* Baby squirrels found helpless on the ground.
* Squirrels that have fallen and hurt themselves.
* Squirrels that have eaten something that does not agree with them (been poisoned).

Squirrels that have been attacked by other animals or run over usually run away or are found dead.

It is not usually possible to examine an adult wild squirrel thoroughly while it is conscious unless it is in a crushable cage or handling cone. Therefore, if there is any doubt about its condition, avoid handling it and let your veterinary surgeon examine it. However, you can do a fair amount for most squirrels that fall into the three main groups needing treatment.

The care of baby squirrels and poisoned squirrels is considered in the following pages. Squirrels that have fallen and hurt themselves usually have concussion (brain shaking), contusion (bleeding and cell death), or compression (pressure due to bleeding) of the brain. Rarely do they need treatment for broken bones and open wounds; if the squirrel is well enough to move about it usually disappears up a tree.

When looking at a new squirrel casualty, wear gloves and spray with an insecticide that will not harm it (a bird spray is most suitable) to get rid of any external parasites. Remember that any baby squirrel taken into care will need toileting (see page 55). This is a very simple process, but the animal will die if it is not done.

Homeopathy

The word *homeopathy* means the treatment of disease by using small amount of a drug that, in healthy persons, produces symptoms similar to those being treated.

It is best to consider all available treatments and to start with those known to have been successful in the past. The course of treatment should always be discussed fully with a vet.

 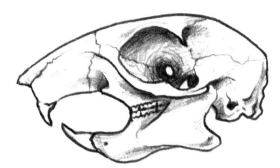

Comparison of the skulls of a Red Squirrel (left) and a Grey Squirrel (right)

The following homeopathic preparations have been found helpful by some carers in treating animals and birds:

Aconite	-	for shock
Arnica	-	for traumatised animals
Calcarea phosphorica	-	for the healing of broken bones
Carbo-vegetabilis	-	for the revival of 'almost dead' animals
Hypericum	-	for pain relief after surgery. (On no account should this be used instead of anaesthetic.)

Homeopathic remedies generally come as tablets, the usual dosage being one tablet of 200 strength daily. The tablet can be crushed and added to the food.

Quick guide to illnesses and symptoms
(For full details see **Alphabetical list of common ailments and their treatments**)

Bald patches	-	Suspect ringworm/mange mites. Isolate.
Broken bones	-	Seek veterinary assistance.
Cold to the touch	-	Warm on heating pad or other heat source.
Coughing	-	Suspect worms or disease. It may have a cold.
Watery eyes and/or discharge from mouth or nose and diarrhoea	-	Suspect disease. Isolate and seek veterinary assistance.
Wobbling, shivering, cold to the touch	-	Suspect dehydration. Offer kitten/puppy milk and milk-soaked bread. Warm on heating pad or other heat source.
Twitching spasms	-	Suspect poisoning.
Unconsciousness/sickness	-	Suspect a fall with resultant head injury.

sciurorum) and parapoxvirus. Red Squirrels, rather than the Greys, are susceptible to parapoxvirus. Both these diseases are common in a range of wildlife.

In Red Squirrels, parapoxvirus causes loss of hair, blindness, conjunctivitis and nasal discharge. The main symptom is conjunctivitis, which makes the eyelids become puffy and swollen and the eyes run. It can be confused with myxomatosis. During 1995 the re-introduction programme for Red Squirrels in England had to be halted because of that disease.

Viral diseases are not usually treatable and the animal is generally destroyed. However, some animals do recover with intense nursing. Veterinary advice is needed and no animal should be released if there is any risk to the wild population.

Anyone who keeps pigeons will be familiar with coccidiosis, which causes diarrhoea (often bloody), general wasting and weakness. It is usually controlled by treating the drinking water.

Other diseases in squirrels have been recorded, including leporipoxvirus (which causes skin tumours and lesions), encephalitis, plague, tularemia pasteurellosis and yersiniosis. These are uncommon and, while yersiniosis and plague can also affect humans, squirrels are not considered of significance in their transmission to humans. Nevertheless, if an unknown disease is suspected, extra hygiene is necessary and you should consult your vet.

Squirrels also suffer from cancers and congenital conditions, and the squirrel that has found its way to you could be the runt of the brood. However, even if you cannot save a squirrel, you can ease its suffering.

Parasites: Parasites are found on (external parasites) and in (internal parasites) healthy squirrels. They are usually a problem only when the animal's resistance is low and the number of parasites increases excessively. They can be grouped as follows:

- External parasites   -   Mites, ticks, lice, fleas, flies.
- Internal parasites   -   Worms (including roundworms, tapeworms, threadworms, flukes and spiny-headed worms). Other organisms.

Although squirrels are very clean animals, they usually carry a few fleas. Sometimes they also carry other parasites such as ticks, mites and lice. Therefore it is best to spray them with a suitable insecticide when you take them into care. A bird spray is quite suitable.

A baby squirrel asleep on a heating pad. It looks as if it is sucking its toes.

A hand-reared squirrel enjoying the relative freedom of an aviary.

The Red and the Grey Squirrel each has its very own flea. For the Red Squirrel it is *Monopsyllus sciurorum* and for the Grey Squirrel it is *Orchopeas howardii*. Although they are generally species specific, they may hop onto domestic animals and humans. The reverse is common; dogs are often blamed for infecting squirrels!

Squirrels kept in outside housing should be treated routinely for parasites.

Mites can cause a loss of fur (alopecia). Mange mites cause sore patches where the fur is absent and the skin appears dandruffy and dusty. It is uncommon in squirrels.

Suspect internal parasites if the squirrel is coughing.

Coccidiosis, which is a form of enteritis, has been mentioned under diseases. The causative organism is a protozoon.

Poisoning: Any sudden large-scale death of animals should be reported and poisoning suspected. The usual treatment for poisoning in squirrels is the same as for dehydration: plenty of kitten/puppy milk formula and water for a few days, the animal being kept very warm. Kaolin products can be added to food and may alleviate the effects of poisoning.

Ringworm: Ringworm is caused by a fungus. Most types of fungus causing ringworm will glow under ultra-violet light. The fur falls out and the skin flakes. However, loss of fur may also be caused by mites (alopecia). Such infections are not normally problematic and I have never had a fatality as a direct result of these conditions. However, if ringworm is suspected, it should be treated. It is contagious and could develop into a serious condition if the animal were already weakened by another disability and the stress of confinement.

Squirrels get a form of ringworm that affects the ears, caused by *Microsporum cokkei*. It causes crusty and flaky ears, but afflicted animals do not seem unduly bothered.

Teeth problems: The front teeth (incisors) will continue to grow throughout the squirrel's life. This is useful for the squirrel as the teeth wear quickly through constant gnawing. On rare occasions, a squirrel's upper and lower teeth may not meet to grind against each other, so that the teeth grow longer and longer and spiral round. If this is left unchecked, the squirrel will die, as it will not be able to eat. Such teeth need regular cutting, and an afflicted squirrel should not be released.

Occasionally squirrels' teeth may break through biting very hard objects. Such teeth usually grow again.

CHAPTER 6

Faced with a choice between peanuts and ice-cream, this squirrel took the ice-cream.

Squirrels are especially fond of chocolate and ice-cream. Once, when we were having a picnic, a squirrel ran up to my daughter and stole a chocolate bar out of her hand as she was about to eat it. It must have watched and waited until she had unwrapped it! Urban squirrels often seek out discarded ice creams and can often be seen sitting on dustbins enjoying cornets in the summer.

For long-term captive squirrels and pets you can buy proprietary rodent food from a pet shop. Food sold for pet rats, gerbils and ferrets is suitable.

Green foods are nibbled in small quantities but squirrels do not eat much. Lettuce, cabbage and carrots can be offered. They also accept fruit. My squirrels take a few bites out of their apples and then carefully store them in their nests. They enjoy fresh berries, such as raspberries, and some dried fruits. Mushrooms can be given to them regularly.

Aim for a varied diet and do not be afraid to offer table scraps, as these are what urban squirrels eat in the wild. They enjoy small quantities of buns, cakes, biscuits and bread with butter, peanut butter or chocolate spread. Feeding young squirrels exclusively on peanuts and dried fruit can lead to rickets.

Squirrels are extremely fussy about the condition of nuts. Avoid collecting forest nuts for captive squirrels. Firstly, if they are sick they may not be strong enough to crack hard shells; secondly, they will not eat them if they are unripe. Some unripe nuts are poisonous. Squirrels do not eat conkers. It is safe to offer walnuts and almonds to squirrels that are reasonably well.

Small quantities of poultry pellets will be accepted, but my squirrels turn their little noses up completely when offered any form of grain. Some workers have seen them eat maize, wheat and sunflower seeds, however.

Give your squirrel a bowl of fresh water every day. Use heavy-duty, non-tip cat bowls, and avoid very large ones; as the squirrel tends to walk through them, it could end up very wet!

Force feeding

Occasionally it might be necessary to force feed a squirrel. The following method can only be used if the squirrel is conscious and able to swallow.

Use a syringe with a small piece of rubber tubing fitted to the end. Support the squirrel upright and gently force the syringe into its mouth. Be careful not to damage

This little one already seems to be trying to use its hands.

Warm and full, this small squirrel sleeps contentedly.

its teeth and do avoid being bitten. (Anyone regularly handling squirrels should keep their tetanus inoculations up to date.) Usually the syringe can be introduced into the side of the mouth, avoiding the large front teeth.

Kitten/puppy milk formula is adequate. Drip the milk onto the squirrel's tongue and watch it swallow. It should lap up the milk as you drip it, but take care not to let the milk drip too quickly. If the squirrel begins to cough, stop immediately. After feeding, wipe away any milk that has run down its belly.

If the animal is too ill to feed in this way, and it really needs to be fed, the only answer is to stomach feed. Lubricate the tube with some cooking oil and slip it down the throat to the stomach. Only give a small amount and avoid squeezing the squirrel; otherwise the animal could regurgitate the fluid and drown. For this reason it may be best to use a semi-solid food. Tins of baby beef dinners are suitable. Use about 0.2ml glucose water (a teaspoon of glucose or sugar in half a cup of water) can be administered if you need to revive an animal.

Although Grey Squirrels are tree squirrels, they spend a lot of time on the ground.

Hand rearing baby squirrels

Where possible, avoid hand rearing pinkies (squirrels up to about three weeks old). If babies are found in a felled tree or a loft that is being converted, leave them for a while. A mother that has been disturbed may return and take them away to a new home. If a very young furred squirrel has fallen from the nest, its mother may attempt to retrieve it. Assess each case individually, remembering that urban baby squirrels do not survive long with cats around or if they are out in the rain.

Pinkies are best kept in incubators or on heating pads at about 30°C. When in doubt, keep young squirrels on heating pads; they are very susceptible to cold. Once furred, squirrels are quite easy to rear by hand, provided that they are found before starvation, dehydration and hypothermia have set in. Starving squirrels need intensive care and take several days to recover. Even when they appear to be doing well the first day they sometimes die the next.

Sterilisation of utensils is unnecessary for furred animals but, for pinkies, it is important to sterilise feeding utensils before and after each feed, just as for a human baby. When using powdered milk, make it up with previously boiled water. Kitten/puppy milk formula is quite suitable. In an emergency goat's milk can be used but, if this is pasteurised, it will need to be boiled first. Milk should be offered at room temperature.

The table below gives a guide to the main constituents of various milks.

	Grey Squirrel	Cow	Goat	Cat
Solids (% dry matter)	40	12	13	27
Fat*	67	26	35	28
Protein*	20	26	25	40
Carbohydrate*	10	39	35	27

* as % solids

As you can see from this table, squirrel milk is very high in fat and solids and relatively low in carbohydrate. When rearing baby squirrels, it is best to use the closest milk to that of squirrels. Although there are considerable differences between kitten or puppy milk formula and squirrel milk, it is the best sterile, easily available option, and it works adequately.

Kitten feeding bottles can be bought from pet shops and veterinary surgeries, and tiny teats from pet supply stores. Make three holes in the end of each teat, using a red-hot needle. A needle can also be used to enlarge and unblock holes. Boil the teats before use. Use old teats whenever possible, as constant re-boiling softens the rubber, making it

Weigh your young squirrels regularly to make sure they are gaining weight.

easier for the animal to suck effectively. Tiny teats can be fitted onto sterile syringes or bottles. If you are using a syringe, and the animal is sucking, the plunger can be removed once the syringe has been filled with milk.

If the baby refuses the milk, check that both milk and animal are warm. Check also whether the squirrel needs toileting (see page 55).

If the animal cannot suck, milk flow through the teat will need careful control from the syringe. Squirrels that already have fur lap the milk rather than suck it. This is fine as long as you watch the animal drinking and, as soon as it stops, stop feeding. Once the animal is used to lapping from a syringe the rubber or teat on the end of it is unnecessary. I find that squirrels with their eyes open take very easily to syringes. The squirrel holds it as you feed it. They have poor coordination and close vision, however, and may miss the syringe when they try to grab it.

When squirrels eat peanuts they usually discard the shells and brown 'skins'.

A word of warning: if you are unsure, it is better to underfeed a little rather than overfeed. Unfortunately I know of many people who have lost baby squirrels by overfeeding them.

The following table is a guide to the amount of milk to give:

Squirrel's age	Amount
Newborn to 1 week	0.1–0.5ml Feed every 2 hours by day and every 3 hours by night.
1–3 weeks	0.5–1ml Increase feeding intervals.
3–5 weeks	2–4ml Feed every 4 hours during the day and wean.

When you start to feed during the daytime only, give the last feed just before you go to bed and feed again first thing in the morning. It is best to feed any sickly animal, whatever its age, during the night. All newly-arrived animals also benefit from a night feed. It is often the runt of the litter that finds its way into human hands, and these animals especially benefit from extra care.

Captive squirrels can be weaned very quickly. I can wean them in a much shorter time than they take in the wild, usually within a few days of their teeth appearing. As soon as you see the teeth growing offer a shallow bowl of milk (kitten or puppy formula) with pieces of bread soaked in it. Offer the bread directly from the hand so that the squirrel can take it in its paws. Because of their poor coordination and close vision, you will need to hand it to them the first few times. They are quick learners if you give them what they enjoy eating. Offer peanuts, complete dried cat food, rodent pet food, and bread-and-butter. Once they are weaned, offer a bowl of milk until the teeth have developed properly and they can eat a range of solid foods.

Once the squirrel has been weaned it can be housed in an open cage with a little nest box (see Chapter 4). Contented baby squirrels will sleep between feeds. You can usually tell when to feed them, as they wake up when they are hungry.

Even after weaning the young squirrel spends some time sleeping during the day. This is normal. However, periods of sleep should be interspersed with periods of high activity. If a youngster is playful, you can be sure that it is doing reasonably well. It should start to groom itself at a couple of months old. Be warned that it will quite happily gnaw through plastic containers.

Toileting

Wipe the squirrel's nose after each feed. Then take a moist tissue and tickle its genitals to stimulate it to urinate and defecate. This process is called 'toileting', and the animal could die if it is not carried out. Toileting is usually unnecessary once the baby is furred (it is usually unnecessary once it is 10–12 days old) but if there is any doubt it is best to continue until the animal is weaned.

Releasing
SQUIRRELS

Young squirrels are charming, gentle explorers.

Unfortunately there is a problem with the release of squirrels. Technically, it is against the law to release Grey Squirrels. With Red Squirrels, it is best to obtain expert advice; they are only likely to survive in certain areas. Many Grey Squirrels have escaped from wildlife care centres. Adult Red Squirrels should be returned to where they were found.

Baby squirrels become tame when they are hand reared. They are intelligent and come to you when they hear your voice. They are trusting and naïve about the dangers in the wild. Wild juvenile squirrels spend several weeks getting used to their surroundings and neighbouring squirrels before permanently leaving the nest. Juveniles not known to neighbouring squirrels may be chased away, and trusting squirrels are easy prey for cats. I know of a squirrel that was attacked by a cat within

A winter drey with some conifer twigs attached.

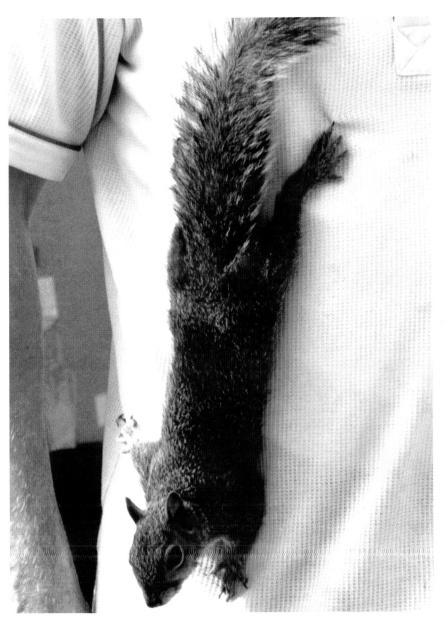

Note the back feet of this squirrel as it hangs upside-down. The back feet have rotated and the toes point upwards.

30 minutes of its release. It returned to its releaser, but died a couple of days later. Consequently, although they may not have the benefit of a slow release, it is probably better to release squirrels in areas with plenty of cover, many trees, a water source and, above all, no cats! As squirrels are intelligent, you may like to visit the release site daily and feed your charge. If you do this at a regular time every day you will probably find your furry friend waiting for you if it is not chased away by other squirrels.

You need to remember that Red Squirrels do not normally thrive in Grey Squirrel areas and cope better in conifer forests, where they can find the food they prefer. You could possibly release juvenile Red Squirrels under a controlled releasing programme.

Do remember also that Red and Grey Squirrels have both caused problems for commercial foresters. It would be irresponsible to release squirrels into forests where they are considered pests.

Partially-sighted and blind squirrels have a diminished probability of survival because of the need to judge distances for jumps. Never release blind animals, and think very carefully about the partially-sighted ones. They make good pets and can live for about 10 years in captivity. Squirrels with one back leg missing could possibly cope, and I have heard of some squirrels coping reasonably well with one front leg missing. Obviously their long-term survival chances are diminished. Tails are used for balance and to signal to other squirrels, so it follows that the squirrel's ability to survive without one would be diminished. Each case, and the availability of a release site, needs individual assessment.

You can release squirrels any time of the year but it is best to avoid bitter winter months and summer droughts. You should release juveniles in the autumn if possible. Above all, it is vital to release them as soon as is practical after they are a couple of months old. If they are with you much longer they could lose all their 'wild' instincts and become pets.

Any squirrel ready for release must be fully acclimatised. That means that it should have been living in an outside cage for some days. Never release a squirrel directly from a heated room to a cold outside environment. They cannot tolerate temperature changes of more than a few degrees at a time.

Finally, although I have never seen it documented before, mention should be made of the squirrel's claws. Hand-reared juveniles behave like cats in the sense that they avoid scratching you. Squirrels need very sharp claws for climbing, but hand-reared squirrels crawl all over you without scratching. They seem to hold the claws differently. When they climb trees, they need to dig them into the trunks. Consequently, before you release your squirrel do make sure that it is climbing well.

Enjoy looking after your garden squirrel, then. If all goes well, it will probably reward you with more baby squirrels for your garden!

A Grey Squirrel in characteristic pose, eating a peanut.

Bibliography

BJARVALL, A *and* ULLSTROM, S **The Mammals of Britain and Europe**; translated by Ernest Neal. London and Sydney: Crook Helm, 1986

BOUCHARDY, C *and* MOUTOU, F **Observing British and European Mammals**; translated by Iain Bishop. London: British Museum (Natural History), 1989

GURNELL, J **The Natural History of Squirrels**. (Christopher Helm Mammal series) 1987

HOLM, J **Squirrels**. London: Whittet Books, 1987

KING, D **Hedgehog in your garden**. Kingdom Books, 1996

LAIDLER, K **Squirrels in Britain**. London: David and Charles, 1980

Useful Addresses

Department of the Environment
Tollgate House
Houlton Street
Bristol   BS2 9DJ   (Tel: 01179 878000)

International Union for the Conservation of Nature
rue Mauverney 28
CH-1196 Gland
Switzerland

Ministry of Agriculture, Fisheries and Food (MAFF)
Whitehall Place
London   SWIA 2HH   (Tel: 0171 273 3000)

Wildlife Trusts
The Green
Witham Park
Waterside South
Lincoln   LN5 7JR   (Tel: 01522 544400)

RSPCA
Causeway
Horsham
West Sussex   RH12 1HG   (Tel: 01403 264181)
National Helpline   (Tel: 0990 555999)

St Tiggywinkles
Wildlife Hospital Trust
Aston Road
Haddenham
Buckinghamshire HP17 8AF (Tel: 01844 292292)

Index

Index